Revealing God

George Arkhurst

Published by Gloripub
Printed in the U.S.A
Copyright © 2019 George Arkhurst
Unless otherwise indicated, the Bible quotations are taken from the from the King James Bible. Request for information should be addressed to:
ISBN-13: 9781703210446

Dedication

T This book is dedicated to my beloved wife, Fatmata
J. Lewally-Arkhurst and our awesome children, Fanta,
Cassandra, Sade and George Jr.

Table of Contents

Dedication   iii

Acknowledgments.   vii

Preface   ix

God Revealed to Man.   1

Introduction of gods   13

The Effect of gods on Earth   25

A Strategy in Play   47

Revealing God in Our Time   69

My Summation.   91

My Challenge to You!   95

Acknowledgments.

All glory and honor be to God Almighty, who had seen me through another inspired writing by His divine grace and mercy, and for His continuing guidance in my life. My parents the late Mr. Jerry Kwesi Arkhurst and Mrs. Cassandra Arkhurst. My Pastor, Rev. Benjamin Boakye, head pastor of Ebenezer Assembly of God church in the Bronx, NY for his continual support in ministry. My wife who is a voice of reasoning, wanting to bring the very best out of me in all my works. My daughter, Fanta who had always helped with proofreading. To Pastor Emmanuel Ekow Yawson a fellow Minister and friend for his support in Ministry. To my very good friends, Bro. and Mrs. Ernest Edmonson Riddle: Bro

Edmonson for his insight and reasoning that greatly helped shape the presentation of the book, his wife Lydia Riddle, the first to help with editing the book. To my friend, my brother and French teacher, Bro Michael Koroma who edited the whole manuscript back and forth a few times. Pastor Mark Asante Manu, who had helped promote my first two publications. To Pastor Samuel Konteh, whose friendship and support I am enjoying. To Pastor Judith Saccoh, my own sister, friend and an able gospel Minister whom I cherish. To my able Superintendent and brother who is a constant help and inspiration. To my good friend, my brother, bro Tony Aghamiogie who had always been my compass giving insights in each book I have written thus far. To my able brother, my friend the one and only bro Eric Asiedu. To Mr. and Mrs. Joshua Elliot an avid promoter of my publications. To all of you brothers and sisters in the Lord at Ebenezer and beyond. God richly bless you all.

Preface

When we hear the name God, it generally conveys certain attributes to mind. Almost everyone living in this world knows about God and have certain expectations by which he or she defines God in his or her mind. It is man's perceived notion that God is good, (He is good). It is man's perception amongst other things that God is straight-forward with no confusion or variations at all. That He is peaceful and promotes peace amongst His creation. But what we see in our world is the total opposite of what our expectations of God are, we see a whole lot of confusion, there had been fights and more fighting going on even now as I am writing this, all in the name of God. And how are these confusions made manifest? They manifest through religion.

Religion is that which is supposed to instruct, to reveal and to keep God's presence on earth very lively. Religion should be that which reveals the God of unity and His desire for people to come together in worship and adoration of Him, but what we are witnessing in our world is the total opposite of such expectations. First, we see that the practice and doctrines of all the religious bodies in our world differ from each other. One teaches that which is directly opposite of what another religious body teaches yet they proclaim it is coming from God. It would have been very clear and understandable if these religious bodies indicate that they all have their own gods and that they want non-religious people to know which of these gods is true and should be worshipped, but none of them are saying that. On the contrary, they all believe they are serving the same God. If that is not confusion, tell me what is? How can God whom we all perceived to be true tell groups of people things that differs from each other about Him? Religion has brought us more confusion than it has clarity. It might make one wonder if God is still with us. The truth is God is still with us and He desires that we find and worship Him. *"And ye shall seek me, and find me, when ye shall search for me with all your heart." Jerimiah 29:13.*

Knowing what was happening in the past and that which is happening now, God made the declaration quoted above for us to know that somehow in this religious world of ours, we have lost sight of Him but that He can be found. God desires that people like you and me find Him in this religious melee of ours. If you don't believe we are in a religious melee tell me why people fight and kill each other in the name of religion? If we are all serving the same God, there will be unity and not division.

I am not sure how many books are out there looking into this, but this book gives an insight into what's happening in the religious world. It is one with arguments, and questions that pricks the mind and causes one to think and to do the arithmetic. Deducing facts from imaginations to be able to make an informed decision on God and religion.

Chapter One

God Revealed to Man.

Initial Revelation.

Generally, humans hold onto the belief that there is God, and this belief or awareness is not something humans discovered through researches, studies or any other human means; it is one that originated from God Himself. The creation story in the Bible explained how God created the world and that man was a part of that creation. *"In the beginning God created the heavens and the earth." Genesis 1:1.* It is recorded that man was made after God's image and likeness. Somehow in His plan, God purposely created man with certain features that will enable him to know, to love and relate to Him. The whole dynamics was for a love relationship between God and man.

Since man was created, there was no way he could have known God before his creation, so it is safe to say that at their first meeting, God introduced Himself to man. *"Then the LORD God formed a man from the dust of the ground and breathed into his nostrils the breath of life, and the man became a living being." Genesis 2:7*. Adam stood up with admiration in his eyes as he beheld God and all His glory. What a sight that must have been. I imagine God took Adam on a tour, engaged him in their first conversation, in which I believe He told him of His love for him and how they should relate to each other. God showed Adam all His handy works and eventually placed him in a beautiful garden called Eden. Adam was struck with awe; he saw the beauty of the world firsthand. His amazement was beyond description, he could not help but notice that creation itself speaks of God. I imagine him bowing in worship to his creator, the great and mighty God.

Through their daily or routine interactions, Adam acquired a complete and thorough knowledge of God to the extent of the revelation of God he got as they related to each other. However, at some point in their walk together, Adam failed God woefully by disobeying Him. God had placed many trees in the Garden and told Adam he can eat from all of them except one, the tree of the knowledge of good and evil.

> *"And the LORD God commanded the man, "You are free to eat from any tree in the garden; but you must not eat from the tree of the knowledge of good and evil, for when you eat from it you will certainly die." Genesis 2:16-17.*

Adam kept his side of the bargain and stayed away from that tree until one fateful day. Scripture says his wife, Eve, got tempted and ate from that tree and she, in turn, gave the fruit to Adam who also ate, breaking God's law and put a strain on their relationship.

"Now the serpent was more crafty than any of the wild animals the LORD God had made. He said to the woman, "Did God really say, 'You must not eat from any tree in the garden'?"² The woman said to the serpent, "We may eat fruit from the trees in the garden, ³ but God did say, 'You must not eat fruit from the tree that is in the middle of the garden, and you must not touch it, or you will die.'"⁴ "You will not certainly die," the serpent said to the woman. ⁵ "For God knows that when you eat from it your eyes will be opened, and you will be like God, knowing good and evil."⁶ When the woman saw that the fruit of the tree was good for food and pleasing to the eye, and also desirable for gaining wisdom, she took some and ate it. She also gave some to her husband, who was with her, and he ate it." Genesis 3:1-6

Throughout his years in the garden, Adam had always been comfortable in God's presence. According to the scriptures, it seemed God would come down to see Adam from time to time. There are two separate accounts mentioned in the Bible regarding that. The first, was when God brought his wife Eve to him and the second was after he had disobeyed God. At that first meeting, Adam was excited to see God because He had brought him a special gift; He had brought him his wife! *"Then the LORD God made a woman from the rib he had taken out of the man, and he brought her to the man. The man said, "This is now bone of my bones and flesh of my flesh; she shall be called 'woman,' for she was taken out of man."* Genesis 2: 22-23. Imagine, Adam's joy and his gratitude to God when he received his wife from Him. He was thankful to God for their continual relationship, he had cherished every moment of it until things took turn for the worse. The scripture recorded that at God's second visit to Adam, he was not that excited because he had disobeyed God and had instantly felt the repercussion of his disobedience. He knew he had lost something, and he no longer felt complete as he used to be. An uncomfortable feeling sets in.

God Separated.

After Adam's disobedience, the dynamics in their relationship changed. Before that, Adam knew God and did not need to be taught how to worship Him. He had a direct open line of communication with Him. There was no confusion as to who God is and how to identify Him. There were no commandments about foreign gods. God was revealed to Adam in perfection. There was a relationship between them, but all of that changed when Adam ate from the forbidden tree, an instant separation occurred, a strange and unrecognized feeling came over him, he knew he had done a terrible thing, disobeying God. He realized that his position had shifted, he felt guilty, restless, and fearful for the first time in his life.

Being separated from God, Adam's perception became tainted, he no longer saw the loving God he had known since his creation but had become fearful of Him. Fearful to the extent that he felt he can no longer be in God's presence, so he hid himself when God came down to visit him.

> *"Then the man and his wife heard the sound of the LORD God as he was walking in the garden in the cool of the day, and they hid from the LORD God among the trees of the garden. But the LORD God called to the man, "Where are you?" He answered, "I heard you in the garden, and I was afraid because I was naked; so I hid."* *Genesis 3:8-10.*

Adam, who used to be in God's company suddenly became fearful of Him and anticipated something he had never known of God, His judgment! He was indeed judged by God and was driven out of the garden. Driven from the home he once knew, the place he often met God, the place where Adam was first introduced to God. A place that held so many memories, a place where a love relationship was established. A place where Adam lost it all.

> *So the LORD God banished him from the Garden of Eden to work the ground from which he had been taken. After*

he drove the man out, he placed on the east side of the Garden of Eden cherubim and a flaming sword flashing back and forth to guard the way to the tree of life. Genesis 3:23-24

Being banished from the garden, Adam finds himself in a strange place. A place of uncertainty, a place where there was no fellowship with God. He felt left alone, confused and scared. He was no longer in God's presence and as such, **he lost that perfect knowledge of God** he had before. To better understand what that was like for Adam, let's liken their relationship to a married couple. A husband will not know his wife until they got introduced and eventually got married to each other. After marrying they will stay together and will grow to know each other very well. But if suddenly, an issue arises that leads to a divorce, one of them will have to leave the house and be separated from the other. This couple that once knew each other well, will become strangers to each other again.

Living together in relationships allows people to know each other very well, but the minute there is a separation, that knowledge will be gone. They will not forget the person they had once been with, but they will not know them like it was when they were together. They will not know how much they have changed since their separation. Because their relationship has been severed, their knowledge of each other diminishes. That was what happened when Adam sinned. Because Adam was kicked out of the garden, he lost that perfect knowledge of God he had before. And the effect of that knowledge lost is rippling down the sea of the earth's population to this day.

The Effect of the Separation.

Though Adam's sin tainted the knowledge of God he had, he was the sole custodian of that knowledge and had the responsibility to pass it down to the next generation. And because his perception had been tainted, it was evidently clear that it affected how he portrayed God when he handed down that knowledge to his sons. Cain's perception of God was different from Abel's. They had learned about God from their father Adam and right at that initial stage, we see the outcome of how they perceived God. They both intended to worship God, which is the right thing to do, but Cain got it wrong. The sacrifice he offered to God was rejected whereas Abel's was accepted. Why did he get it wrong and why did Abel get it right? Because they both perceived God differently based on how they understood Him from Adam.

> *"Now Abel kept flocks, and Cain worked the soil. In the course of time Cain brought some of the fruits of the soil as an offering to the LORD. [4] And Abel also brought an offering—fat portions from some of the firstborn of his flock. The LORD looked with favor on Abel and his offering, but on Cain and his offering he did not look with favor. So, Cain was very angry, and his face was downcast. Then the LORD said to Cain, "Why are you angry? Why is your face downcast? If you do what is*

right, will you not be accepted? But if you do not do what is right, sin is crouching at your door; it desires to have you, but you must rule over it." Genesis 4:2-7

In the scripture above, God had a dialogue with Cain, in which He admonished him *"if you do what is right, will you not be accepted?" Genesis 4:7.* I believe that Cain had intended to please God, he did the best he could as he saw fit. But we see that God did not accept his offering. That was because he got it all wrong, he was not doing it God's way. The Cain effect had been happening since that first incident. Throughout all generations, man has sought different ways to worship God and had taught others to do so. Some like Abel understood and worshipped God correctly, while others, like Cain, understood wrongly and so miss the standard God had set to worship Him.

Experience has taught us that an incident reported down a line of several individuals, tends to change as it goes down the line. This theory holds in man's ways of worshipping God. Humans have deduced a variation of forms and methods to worship Him due to the hand me down information system. People's perception of Him has degenerated to the extent that they changed the glory of God to look like images.

> *"For although they knew God, they neither glorified him as God nor gave thanks to him, but their thinking became futile and their foolish hearts were darkened. Although they claimed to be wise, they became fools and exchanged the glory of the immortal God for images made to look like a mortal human being and birds and animals and reptiles." Romans 1.21-23*

Chapter Two

Introduction of gods

P rior to Adam's sin, there was no knowledge of foreign gods. The God of heaven was the only God known to man. But after man sinned, foreign gods became a part of our world and had consequently become man's object of worship. All through the scriptures are instances of idol worship and God's warnings against such practices. Matter of fact, the first of the commandments God gave to man has to do with idol worship. *"Thou shall have no other gods before me" Exodus 20:3.* Who are these gods and where do they come from? Why do people worship them anyway?

Understanding who or what these gods are will greatly help people make informed decision as to who they worship. Understanding their nature and existence is of great essence if one is to be informed and be knowledgeable in terms of directing one's worship in the right direction. The scriptures give adequate insights that help reveal who these gods are. When the Apostle Paul was writing his first letter to the Corinthian Church, he alluded to the fact that there are many gods in the world. *"For even if there are so-called gods, whether in heaven or on earth (as indeed there are many gods and many lords). 1Corinthians 8:5.* And in his second letter to the same Church, he referred to a specific god. *"In whom* **_the god_** *of this world has blinded the minds of them which believe not…"* *2Corinthians 4:4a* Note that the Apostle used the definite article 'the' referring to this god. He said, *"the god of this world" 2Corinthians 4:4.*

Notice how the Apostle referred to the gods in the referenced scriptures, in one of them, Paul said, the god, meaning a specific god and then in the other he said there are many gods. By these scriptures, we can safely categorize the gods of this world into two, 'all other gods' and "the god of this world.' Let us do some comparing for a clear and more thorough understanding of all the gods.

The god of this World.

Who is this god that is referred to as the god of this world and why is he called by that name? It is clear from the scriptures that God had created angelic beings before He created this world. The Bible did not tell us when and how, but as man lived and interacted with God, we discovered that there are angels in the world. The Bible calls them ministering spirits that are sent by God to serve. *"Are not all angels ministering spirits sent to serve those who will inherit salvation?" Hebrews 1:14* One of these angels was Lucifer. From the short account we have of this angel in scriptures, we learned of how he disobeyed and rebelled against God almighty. **He intended to raise himself above God, so he can seat**

as God. But since he was created by God, he does not have the power to overthrow God almighty and so he got tossed out from God's company.

> *How art thou fallen from heaven, O Lucifer, son of the morning! how art thou cut down to the ground, which didst weaken the nations! [13] For thou hast said in thine heart, I will ascend into heaven, I will exalt my throne above the stars of God: I will sit also upon the mount of the congregation, in the sides of the north: I will ascend above the heights of the clouds; I will be like the most High. Isaiah 14:12-14*

From the quoted scripture above, we learn that this rebellious angel was hurled down to earth. And the narrative in the book of Revelation corroborates that account.

> *Then war broke out in heaven. Michael and his angels fought against the dragon, and the dragon and his angels fought back. But he was not strong enough, and they lost their place in heaven. The great dragon was hurled down- -that ancient serpent called the devil, or Satan, who leads*

the whole world astray. He was hurled to the earth, and his angels with him. Revelation 12:7-9

The Bible refers to him as Satan, the old serpent and the devil. It also mentions the fact that he leads the whole world astray. The New Living Translation Bible identifies Satan as the god of this world. *"Satan, who is the god of this world, has blinded the minds of those who don't believe." 2Corinthians 4:4a.* This makes it abundantly clear that "the god of this world" has been identified, we now know that Satan is indeed the god of this world.

All Other gods.

For all the other gods mentioned, the scriptures named quite a few of them. We have names like Baal, Dagon, etc., these gods cannot be traced back to an origin as we did for "the god of this world." They were not created by God, they were man-made gods, carved from wood or stones from man's imagination.

"The carpenter measures with a line and makes an outline with a marker; he roughs it out with chisels and

marks it with compasses. He shapes it in human form, human form in all its glory, that it may dwell in a shrine He cut down cedars, or perhaps took a cypress or oak. He let it grow among the trees of the forest, or planted a pine, and the rain made it grow. It is used as fuel for burning; some of it he takes and warms himself, he kindles a fire and bakes bread. But he also fashions a god and worships it; he makes an idol and bows down to it." Isaiah 44:13-15

Are these idols really God? Do they have the power to do anything at all by themselves? Do you really believe a wood carved out and adorned has the power to protect or provide? If not, why do people build, erect and worship them? Why are people so dedicated to rituals and ceremonies that is done in idol worship? This calls for some deep and sincere pondering to understand why they do such. I had done some pondering myself and came up with a few facts I believe is causing people to worship idols. As we explore these facts, keep in mind that man's perception of God has been tainted since the fall.

I. The Fact that God Exists

Man is cognizant of the existence of God because God created the world in such that there is evidence of His existence throughout. *"The heavens declare the glory of God; the skies proclaim the work of his hands. Day after day they pour forth speech; night after night they reveal knowledge." Psalms 19:1-2*

The above scripture is a declaration that creation is a witness to the fact that there is a higher power that is in control. The way the world is put together reveals the work of a calculated and well thought out plan just like an architect would, in preparing to erect a building. This leaves no doubt that there is someone responsible for Earth's creation. When we observe the constant seasons, the borderlines that keep lands and seas separated, the sunrise and sunset, the animals and plants, and everything in creation, we cannot help but acknowledge the existence of God. There are four or two seasons in the world depending on geographical locations, and these seasons, have never ceased since creation. It is all beautifully designed and executed. Creation is one powerful testament of God's existence that is on display daily in so much that man has no excuse of knowing He exists. *"For since the creation of the world His invisible attributes are clearly seen, being understood by the things that are made, even His eternal power and [a]Godhead, so that they are without excuse. Romans 1:20*

II.   The Fear of God's Judgment

Within every human heart, there is a feeling of unworthiness when it comes to meeting one on one with God, we do not have the confidence to be in His presence. Matter of fact we dread meeting face to face with Him. For you to get what I am portraying here, let's assume God is walking through your living room this minute, calling your name from your front door as He walks towards you, will you be comfortable with that? What would you do?

A colleague of mine once said he might run through the door away from God when asked that question. Why would he run? Because he felt unworthy to be in God's presence. And that unworthy feeling is due to the guilt and condemnation within him which every one of us identifies with, and that feeling terrifies us.

Adam was the first to exhibit that feeling of unworthiness. After he sinned the Bible says he hid himself when he heard God walking in the garden where he was living. Adam became fearful of God; he did not know what God will do to him for disobeying His commandment.

"And they hear the voice of the Lord walking in the garden in the cool of the day and Adam and his wife hid themselves from the presence of the Lord God amongst the trees of the garden." Genesis 3:8.

Adam knew that he had not seen or heard the last from God after he sinned, that knowledge now coupled with fear led him to do something he thought might appease God and avert his punishment. He made clothing with leaves to cover himself. He anticipated that it might be enough to appease God and make him worthy before Him. What Adam did, was the beginning of the formation of man's religion. Since that time to the end of age, man has been and will be finding his own ways to appease God in a bid to make his conscience free from the condemnation he feels when he thinks about facing God. But even after Adam did what he thought might appease God, he hid himself when he heard God's voice in the garden looking for him. He felt unworthy still and was indeed fearful to face God.

That attitude of Adam is found displayed in a narrative recorded in Acts of the Apostle. When Paul went to Athens, during his missionary journey, he saw an array of thousands of gods and shrines that were built by the people of Athens. These people were so fearful of God's wrath that they gather to themselves whatever they perceived to be a deity and make one out of it. Having amassed all these gods, they were still unsure, so they built another altar to the unknown God. I believe they were doing so to satisfy all and everything they perceived to be God. Fearing the wrath they will face if they had left out any.

III.   The Seemingly Prosperity of Idol Worshippers

The third factor is the seemingly prosperous lives of Idol worshippers. People who worship Idols seem to be doing good in this material world. Bible stories record the good life of the Egyptians compared to that of the Israelites. The Egyptians with all their idols were the masters and the Israelites were their slaves. The Israelites did observe the prosperity of the Egyptians, they saw their golds and whatever other earthly wealth they possessed. They watched them live very fine lives by worldly standards. So it was not too hard for them to turn away from God to similar idols the Egyptians worshipped several times in their walk with God.

In an Exodus narrative, the scriptures recorded how Moses a prophet of God was sent to deliver the Israelites from slavery. He was to lead them to a land promised to them by God, this land was fondly called the 'promised land'. Moses got them free and journeyed with them toward that land. But at one point in their journey, he left them and went up a mountain called Sanai. While he was still up the mountain the Israelites became impatient and asked Aaron to make gods for them that will lead them there. *"They said to me, make us gods who will go before us. As for this fellow Moses, we don't know what has happened to him" Exodus 32:23.* They wanted to get to the promised land, and they needed God's guidance to get them there but Moses who had been leading them was nowhere to be found. So they asked Aaron to make them a god because the Israelites had lived amongst the Egyptians and had seen how they prospered serving their gods (idols).

Chapter Three

The Effect of gods on Earth

The above chapter sheds light on the many gods in this world, which I have placed in two categories for a better understanding of their beings, their operations and how they affect our world. As the scripture says and as it is evident, our world is indeed housing many gods, but the knowledge of many gods is either being trivialized or is not thought of by most people.

"For even if there are so-called gods, whether in heaven or on earth (as indeed there are many gods and many lords). 1 Corinthians 8:5

When we think of God, we think about worship. God is supposed to be worshipped; God is supposed to have worshippers who worship Him. So, these many gods have worshippers who worship them and propagate their teachings. Teachings that differ slightly, but sometimes outright contradictory to each other. Yet, every single one of them claims to be the truth and worse yet, is the belief that all these religions formed and practiced are serving the same God. This has left the world in utter chaos and confusion. How can God give a set of rules or commandments to a set of people and something totally different to another? Think about that for a second. If that is not confusing, then tell me what is.

People do have their expectations of God. They expect Him to be truthful, powerful loving and caring to name a few. But with all these different teachings and religious beliefs supposedly coming from God, people are left dumbfounded. I believe this is one reason that gave rise to Atheism. These religious inconsistencies caused some people to not only deduce what seems logical to them but also to propagate their belief that there is no God. This belief also adds to the mix, broadening the existing confusion. How can God be this difficult to find? How can He throw mankind into this vacuous state of searching and researching His whereabouts? Is God really the one behind this confusion? Are all of these religious teachings from Him?

If these teachings differ and they do; is it not possible that some of them are not true and cannot be coming from the same God? We all will agree that if two people have two opposing views of the same thing, it is very likely that one of the views maybe correct while the other may be wrong. God cannot oppose Himself, there is got to be someone else doing that. The Bible says *"let God be true and every man a liar..."Romans 3:4...*

Let's Get Logical

One of the blessings God gave to man is the ability to reason. Man can look at situations and circumstances critically and make logical conclusions of their assessments. But when it comes to seeking God which I believe matters the most, that ability is either not being explored or is being used very inadequately. In our world today, these religious differences and their contradictions are not oblivious, but we do not take time to explore or to find out why there are so many confusions and contradictions in our religious world. So, let's get logical for a moment to see what sense we can make out of this all.

Let us go back to the beginning of times and re-examine the creation story. That story did not mention nor bear records of other gods, it talks of all the things created and at the end of it all, God said it was very good. *"And God saw everything that he had made, and, behold, it was very good..." Genesis 3:31A.* Foreign gods entered the realms of the earth after Adam sinned. We know from scriptures that God and Adam had a perfect relationship until he sinned. From then on, false gods started appearing and have gained significant recognition throughout human history.

In the second chapter of this book, "Introducing the gods of this world," I categorized them into two; the god of this world and all other gods. I referenced how the god of this world can be traced and have biblical records of how he came to be, but all the other gods do not have such records. What we have are records of how they were handcrafted by men and are housed in shrines as objects of worship. *"But their idols are silver and gold, made by human hands.[5] They have mouths, but cannot speak, eyes, but cannot see.[6] They have ears, but cannot hear, noses, but cannot smell.[7] They have hands, but cannot feel, feet, but cannot walk, nor can they utter a sound with their throats. Psalms 115:4-7*

Consequently, because of the inflow of foreign gods we now have God almighty, who **creates** the world, the god of this world and all other gods. This is not to a comparison, but a statement of fact proven from scriptures. God is God and cannot be compared to any other. Now that we have discovered that there are many gods, let's do a little more digging on them in order to come to a logical and wise conclusion that will help us in choosing which to worship.

Identifying the Power of the gods

The scripture has records of powers being demonstrated that are not from God almighty. An example of such power is found in Exodus, the second book of the Bible. In that narrative is an epic demonstration of powers between Moses and Pharaoh. Moses was sent by God almighty to go tell Pharaoh the then Egyptian king to let God's people, the Israelites go. The Israelites had been in bondage to Pharaoh for a long time. In obedience to God Moses accompanied by Aaron went to Pharaoh and told him to let the Israelites go just as God had commanded but Pharaoh refused. He then asked Moses to perform a miracle. It seemed as if Pharaoh either wanted to know if there is any authority or power in Moses or wanted to display his own powers. Moses through Aaron performed a miracle that God had already told him to perform when he would be asked by Pharaoh. He commanded Aaron to drop his staff and it turned to a snake, just as the Lord had commanded. Pharaoh did not seem to be impressed by that he summoned his magicians, they came and dropped their staffs, and all became snakes also.

> *The LORD said to Moses and Aaron "When Pharaoh says to you, 'Perform a miracle,' then say to Aaron, 'Take your staff and throw it down before Pharaoh,' and it will become a snake." So Moses and Aaron went to Pharaoh and did just as the LORD commanded. Aaron threw his staff down in front of Pharaoh and his officials, and it became a snake. Pharaoh then summoned wise men and sorcerers, and the Egyptian magicians also did the same things by their secret arts: Each one threw down his staff and it became a snake. But Aaron's staff swallowed up their staffs. Exodus 7:8-12*

That incident was a spectacle of power to have witnessed. On one end were Moses and Aaron, representatives of God almighty and on the other Pharaoh and his magicians, representatives of an entity that will be revealed through our systematic reasoning in the pages of this book. If any neutral person had witnessed that, I am sure they would have been thrilled and confused at the same time. Thrilled because they would have witnessed powers being demonstrated and confused because they would have wondered which power is which? Wondering if the powers displayed were from God and if so, why did it look like a challenge. Can God challenge Himself like that? Something worth pondering.

It is clear from the Moses-Pharaoh narrative above that power was displayed at that encounter, on one end was God's power demonstrated by His servant Moses and on the other end was Pharaoh's magicians. So now, the question is whose power was demonstrated by Pharaoh's magicians? Since the power of Pharaoh's magicians was not from God, we are left with "the god of this world" and "all other gods." In order to determine which of these gods is the power behind the magicians, let us do some comparison of the two categories of gods as put forth in this book. Keep in mind that we had placed these gods into two categories, all other gods and the god of this world. So let's look at few names of all the other gods and see what they did or didn't do and compare that to the "god of this world."

In the scriptures is recorded an incident with one of these gods, called Dagon. Dagon was a carved-out idol that was placed in a temple the Philistines built for it. These Philistines were enemies of Israel. It so happened that, they went to war with Israel, overcame them and captured the Ark of the covenant from the Israelites and brought it into Dagon's temple. This Ark symbolized the presence of the almighty God in the camp of the Israelites. Putting it in Dagon's temple seems like an invitation to a show of power. The following morning when the Philistines came to worship their god, the found it lying down on the floor before the Ark of the covenant. They picked it up and set it to stand upright again. The next morning, they found it on the floor again, this time the head and limbs were broken and detached from its body. Now if Dagon had any power, it could at least pick itself up when it fell. But as is seen here, Dagon, was powerless.

> *"After the Philistines had captured the ark of God, they took it from Ebenezer to Ashdod Then they carried the ark into Dagon's temple and set it beside Dagon.[3] When the people of Ashdod rose early the next day, there was Dagon, fallen on his face on the ground before the ark of the LORD! They took Dagon and put him back in his place. But the following morning when they rose, there was Dagon, fallen on his face on the ground before the ark of the LORD! His head and hands had been broken off and were lying on the threshold; only his body remained.[5] That is why to this day neither the priests of Dagon nor any*

others who enter Dagon's temple at Ashdod step on the threshold." 1 Samuel 5:1-5

Another incident I would refer to is recorded in the book of Kings. It was another power showdown between Elijah the prophet of God and the four hundred prophets of Baal. That was a time in Israel, when people were seemingly confused about religion and how to know and worship the God of heaven. It seemed people were genuinely confused but eager to know if they were on the right path. There was on one hand, the prophet Elijah with one set of teachings, and on the other were the prophets of Baal and those of Asherah with teachings that differed from Elijah's. One day, according to the scriptures, Elijah met with King Ahab and invited him and the whole of Israel to a place called mount Carmel. Elijah intended to show who is God.

"When he saw Elijah, he said to him, "Is that you, you troubler of Israel?" "I have not made trouble for Israel," Elijah replied. "But you and your father's family have.

You have abandoned the LORD's commands and have followed the Baals. Now summon the people from all over Israel to meet me on Mount Carmel. And bring the four hundred and fifty prophets of Baal and the four hundred prophets of Asherah, who eat at Jezebel's table." 1 Kings 18:17-19.

The prophet Elijah threw a challenge to the prophets of Baal in the presence of the whole of Israel.

Then Elijah said to them, "I am the only one of the LORD's prophets left, but Baal has four hundred and fifty prophets. Get two bulls for us. Let Baal's prophets choose one for themselves, and let them cut it into pieces and put it on the wood but not set fire to it. I will prepare the other bull and put it on the wood but not set fire to it. [24] Then you call on the name of your god, and I will call on the name of the LORD. The god who answers by fire—he is God." Then all the people said, "What you say is good." 1 Kings 18:22-24.

This was a solemn time for Elijah and the entire nation of Israel. This narrative depicts human traits when it comes to dealing with God. I have come to understand that the vast majority of humankind has some sort of allegiance to God. What I mean is this, regardless of what faith people practice, no matter what doctrines are taught, there have always been people who are very serious and dedicated to what they believe about God. We have observed people doing all sorts of questionable things in the name of God. In recent times, people had blown themselves up believing they are fulfilling God's will. Others had their leaders ask them to do very questionable things which they had gladly done, thinking they were doing God's will also. What I see in all these is man's desire and willingness to find a way to please God. But is He pleased by these practices? And are people reaching the God they intend to reach?

The scene at Mount Carmel was nothing short of such traits. Two groups of people, each dedicated to what they know and believe was God's way for them. Recognizing their differences in ways of worship, they came to prove which of them was serving the living God! Elijah threw a challenge to the prophets of Baal in the presence of the whole nation of Israel. This was a serious business as some of these Israelites were torn between these two or more religious practices of their days. That day was a day of great importance and all were waiting to know who God is.

Elijah asked that two altars be built for the two sacrifices to be made. One for him and the other for all the prophets of Baal. Elijah asked that the prophets of Baal choose one of the bulls for themselves, cut it accordingly and put it on their altar, but not to set it on fire. He then asked the prophets to call on their god to come down and consume the sacrifice. As is narrated in the scriptures below, the prophets of Baal, cried out to their god for a considerable amount of time. Elijah was even having a field day, taunting them to shout louder. The whole of Israel observed the rituals of

these prophets, cutting themselves with spears in a bid
to please their god but nothing happened.

Elijah said to the prophets of Baal, "Choose one of the
bulls and prepare it first, since there are so many of you.
Call on the name of your god, but do not light the
fire." So they took the bull given them and prepared
it. Then they called on the name of Baal from morning till
noon. "Baal, answer us!" they shouted. But there was no
response; no one answered. And they danced around the
altar they had made. At noon Elijah began to taunt them.
"Shout louder!" he said. "Surely he is a god! Perhaps he
is deep in thought, or busy, or traveling. Maybe he is
sleeping and must be awakened." ²⁸ So they shouted
louder and slashed themselves with swords and spears, as
was their custom, until their blood flowed. ²⁹ Midday
passed, and they continued their frantic prophesying until
the time for the evening sacrifice. But there was no
response, no one answered, no one paid attention. 1 Kings
18:25-29

All the efforts of these prophets did not do bring about the fulfillment of the challenge set up by Elijah that they had agreed to. Since nothing happened during their cry to their god and time is far spent, Elijah then took center stage. He called the people and then set up the altar that he intends to offer his sacrifice upon. Elijah had confidence that he was serving the living God, so he did something out of the ordinary, he asked that water be poured on the sacrifice and the wood underneath it. Elijah then called on the name of the Lord and fire came down from heaven and consumed the sacrifice!

> *Then Elijah said to all the people, "Come here to me."*
> *They came to him, and he repaired the altar of*
> *the* LORD, *which had been torn down. Elijah took twelve*
> *stones, one for each of the tribes descended from Jacob, to*
> *whom the word of the* LORD *had come, saying, "Your*
> *name shall be Israel." With the stones he built an altar*
> *in the name of the* LORD, *and he dug a trench around it*

large enough to hold two seahs of seed. He arranged the wood, cut the bull into pieces and laid it on the wood. Then he said to them, "Fill four large jars with water and pour it on the offering and on the wood." "Do it again," he said, and they did it again. "Do it a third time," he ordered, and they did it the third time. The water ran down around the altar and even filled the trench. At the time of sacrifice, the prophet Elijah stepped forward and prayed: "LORD, the God of Abraham, Isaac and Israel, let it be known today that you are God in Israel and that I am your servant and have done all these things at your command. Answer me, LORD, answer me, so these people will know that you, LORD, are God, and that you are turning their hearts back again." Then the fire of the LORD fell and burned up the sacrifice, the wood, the stones and the soil, and also licked up the water in the trench. When all the people saw this, they fell prostrate and cried, "The LORD—he is God! The LORD—he is God!" 1 Kings 18:30-39

At the end of this showdown, the God of Elijah was declared to be God because His power was revealed, and so the people worshipped Him. Baal, with all the four hundred prophets, could not do a single thing befitting God. It was powerless! God is supposed to have power, He should be able to do miracles and all the impossible things man cannot do. So, when Baal cannot demonstrate any power, we can safely say, it had none! We have now understood that Dagon and Baal, gods that people worshipped are powerless. If we go down the list of every one of "the other gods" we will come to the same conclusion, they are without any power.

> *"The idols of the nations are silver and gold, made by human hands. They have mouths, but cannot speak, eyes, but cannot see. They have ears, but cannot hear, nor is there breath in their mouths Those who make them will be like them, and so will all who trust in them." Psalms 135:15-18*

We have seen and can agree on the fact that "all the other gods" are not capable of doing any powerful or miraculous thing. If these gods categorized under "all other gods" are powerless, it leaves us with the god referred to as "the god of this world." This god is identified as Satan. In fact, the scripture has some choice names for him, but I will only take a few and expound on them for this book.

1. The prince of the power of the air. *"Wherein in time past ye walked according to the course of this world, according to* **the prince of the power of the air***, the spirit that now worketh in the children of disobedience." Eph. 2:2*

This scripture is one of many that ascribes power to Satan, another scripture I will use here to make this fact clear is found in 2nd Thessalonians 2:9, it reads. *" Even him, whose coming is after the* **working of Satan with all power and signs and lying wonders***."* This counts for his ability to do miracles. It is evident that there are displays of power in the world that are not from God. There is a range of powerful activities that I will not get into, so I don't deviate from the topic. I have searched the scriptures and I am yet to find a single verse that ascribes power to any of the other gods named or unnamed in the scriptures. We can now establish that "all other gods" are powerless but the god of this world, on the other hand has power. So, we can conclude that the power behind Pharaoh's magicians was from the god of this world.

In the previous chapter, I have proven from scriptures that idols are powerless. But allow me to point out also that people are worshipping them. We see from scripture how dedicated the prophets of Baal were, cutting themselves and shouting to their god, Baal. Why do these people believe in Baal? Better yet, why do people believe in and worship idols? Throughout the scripture, we have accounts of people worshipping and offering sacrifices to them. Why? Can't humans tell they are wood that they themselves have made? Are men that oblivious or are just plain foolish, to worship and serve these gods? I don't think so. I think humans are very intelligent. They must have seen or have had some proof as to why they continue to worship their various objects of worship. They must have experienced some power being demonstrated which they perceived is from their gods. If they have had such experiences and they have, where do these powers come from? That is the controversial question, a question we need an answer to.

The effect of gods on earth

Chapter Four

A Strategy in Play
1. Hiding Behind Idols

In the preceding chapters, I expounded with scriptural proofs on how all gods in the 'all other gods' category is powerless. I also proved from scriptures that 'the god of this world' on the contrary has some power. I presented the power showdown in Egypt between Moses and Pharaoh's magicians and then posed a question to determine who was behind the power demonstrated by those magicians at Pharaoh's court. I came to the reasonable conclusion that the power behind Pharaoh's magicians was that of the god of this world. However, the magicians in Pharaoh's court did not know that; they were idol worshippers who were convinced without a doubt that whatever power they had perceived, experienced or had benefitted from, came from the idols they worshipped. Idol worshippers believe in their objects of worship, they trust and somehow rely on them. Why? Because, like Pharaoh's magicians, they have somehow seen power they perceived is from them and that justifies their beliefs in them. What they don't know is their gods (idols), like Dagon and Baal are powerless. That whatever powers they have seen displayed or had benefited from, did not actually come from these gods. In Isaiah, there is a fine scripture that alludes to that fact.

> *Bring out the people who have eyes but are blind, who have ears but are deaf. Gather the nations together! Assemble the peoples of the world! Which of their idols has ever foretold such things? Which can predict what will happen tomorrow? Where are the witnesses of such predictions? Who can verify that they spoke the truth? Isaiah 43:8-9*

Idols are powerless, so the power perceived by their worshippers must be coming from another source. In this book, I have presented the sources of power that operates in the world. We all know that the God of the universe is all-powerful, and we've also known that 'the god of this world' has some amount of power. We also know that God is truthful when God demonstrates His power, He wants people to know it's from Him. So, He cannot be the One behind the power that idol worshippers perceived is coming from their idols. Since it is not coming from God, the only other power that is known from the scriptures is the god of this world so we can safely say the perceived powers of idols are from him.

2. Leading the World Astray

*⁹The great dragon was hurled down—that ancient serpent called the devil, or Satan, **who leads the whole world astray**. He was hurled to the earth, and his angels with him.Rev.12:9.*

The scripture says the devil leads the whole world astray. To lead someone astray means to be dishonest with that someone, it means to lie to that person. It means to point him or her in the wrong direction. And the devil is doing just that. He lies convincingly, and people believe his lies. He hides behind the object people carved and installed as gods, causing them to believe that such objects have powers to meet their needs. Jesus called him the father of lies. *"You belong to your father, the devil,...<u>When he lies, he speaks his native language, for he is a liar and the father of lies." </u>John 8:44* Jesus said, when he lies, he is speaking in his native language.

Scriptures also say he is subtle. *"Now the serpent was* **<u>more subtle</u>** *than any beast of the field which the* LORD *God had made... Genesis 3:1a.* With these skills, he is armed to do his bid, leading the whole world astray subtlety with deception.

How he Operates

He operates with words. Understanding the power of words can change a whole dynamic. Words are what causes things to happen. They are spoken to produce good, bad or ugly effects. Say something to a stranger, a family is derived, say something to a stranger and someone is dead. Words produce effects! When we understand what words can accomplish, we will master the art of knowing and using words correctly. Unlike mankind, the devil understands that, he knows words work. He must have seen when God spoke the world into being. He had witnessed the power of words, God's Word. He had seen its effect on earth, so he uses it effectively. Twisting it a little here and a little there, to produce the desired effect on people as he intends.

This strategy of his was revealed in the creation story. The Bible tells us how he went to Eve and asked her a question concerning God's word. *"Now the serpent was more subtle…and he said to the woman, yea, hath God said ye shall not eat of every tree in the garden?" Genesis 3:1* That question got Eve just as the devil might have anticipated. He knew that was not what God said to Adam and Eve but in his subtleness, he took some parts of God's word, twisted it in such that he got her to disobey God.

What God told Adam and Eve was this: *"And the Lord God commanded the man, saying, of every fruit of the garden thou mayest freely eat but of the tree of the knowledge of good and evil thou shalt not eat..."* Genesis 2:16-17. When you look at these two scriptures, you'll see some common traits in them, but when you look more closely, you'll see that they differ. That is how the devil works in getting people to stray from God. He gives them a little of God's word with a twist to it.

If you take a statistic of all major religious texts, most, if not all of them sprung from one source, the Bible. Why? Because the Bible is God's word to man. His entire counsel, His playbook or manual by which man should live on earth. The Bible has authority, so it makes perfect sense to take portions of it to form different belief systems. There are very fine and convincing writers in the world, past, present and future. One could have written scripts and laws to form a religion, but I am not sure if it will last long. There had been a few who tried but they died as quickly as they were formed.

> *"For before these days rose up Theudas, boasting himself to be somebody; to whom a number of men, about four hundred, joined themselves; who was slain; and all as many as obeyed him were scattered and brought to nought. After this man rose up Judas of Galilee in the days of taxing, and drew away much people after him: he also perished and all, even as many as obeyed him were dispersed." Acts 5:36-37.*

These men perished with their followers because their doctrines I believe were of little or no authority at all. But texts that can be relayed to the Bible can be seen and in fact is seen as somewhat authentic.

Consider money with its purchasing power. It is designed in such a way that whoever sees it recognizes it as money and because of its power, people want to get as much of it as they possibly can. Some even go out of the way to make counterfeit currencies. The counterfeit they make are of real currencies that have purchasing power like the dollar or the pound sterling. They do not just make one out of their imagination because it would not produce the desired effect. It will have no background, no authenticity and no purchasing power. Even though it will be defined as money based on its features, it will be useless. When people make counterfeit money, they make one like the dollar because of its power and the possibility that it can be used in the world with good chances of utilizing the purchasing power of the real dollar. It is for that same reason that most if not all religious writings have a good amount from the Bible. They have good amounts of excerpts from the Bible but with a significant amount of additions or changes. These changes or additions vary from slight to direct opposite.

Effects of his Operations

The god of this world, otherwise called, the devil or Satan having successfully deceived Eve with the twisting of God's word, makes that his established pattern to deceive people. Remember his strategy is to take the word of God he had twisted, to a set of people and another set to a different set of people. If you want to prove me wrong, then come up with a sound reason why we have this much religion with different doctrines all claiming to be from God? For a refresher, let's examine how he got Eve to buy into disobeying God. Take note of the words he used on Eve, they contain some of what God actually said to Adam concerning the tree "*Now the serpent was more subtle…and he said to the woman, yea, <u>hath God said ye shall not eat of every tree in the garden?</u>" Genesis 3:1* now that was not what God said to Adam. Here is what God said to Adam: "*And the Lord*

God commanded the man, saying, <u>of every fruit of the garden thou</u> *<u>mayest freely eat</u> but of the tree of the knowledge of good and evil* *thou shalt not eat…" Genesis 2:16-17* Notice the twist by comparing the underlined portions, that is how the devil operates. He twists here and there to get people to sway from the truth, now here are a few examples of what is with us today -:

1. The second commandment from God reads, *"Thou shalt not make unto thee any graven image, or any likeness of anything that is in heaven above, or that is in the earth beneath, or that is in the water under the earth Thou shalt not bow down thyself to them, nor serve them:…"Exodus 20:4-5A* Despite that command, a group of religious bodies have images all over their places of worship with worshippers bowing to the images, going against what God said in His commandment. Where did they get their instructions to do so?

2. Another Scripture says, *"there is one God and one mediator between God and man, the man Christ, Jesus"*

1 Timothy 2:5. But you have millions asking someone else to intercede, pray to God for them now and at the hour of their death.

3. Yet again the Bible says, *"But though we, or an angel from heaven, preach any other gospel unto you than that which we have preached unto you, let him be accursed."* *Galatians 1:8,* yet we have millions of people following doctrines revealed to men who had visitations from angels.

4. Throughout the scriptures are several verses that talk about God's Son. *"...this is my beloved Son, in whom I am well pleased." Mathew 3:17.* While many believe what that scripture says, there is a vast majority of people that believe the contrary. People believe that God does not have a Son.

In each of these examples, we see that God's word is not being followed. We see people doing the exact opposite of what He commands, and they do so with reverence as unto God. But if God did not command them to do so, why are they doing that? Do people just choose to blatantly disobey God? Not exactly, as I said earlier, humans have an allegiance toward God and will never in their right minds want to disobey Him. But we see and know that people build these images and because they do, they are in disobedience to God. We have also argued that man in his right mind will not blatantly disobey God. If this is happening and it is, it calls for one to re-examine and make a conscious decision whether to keep worshiping those images or bowing to them or kneeling to them.

Like those who build images in their sanctuaries, there is another set of people who claimed to have had visitations from angels with what they believed to be God's message for the world, even though the scripture had warned concerning that. The Bible says even if an angel from heaven should preach **any other** gospel, he should be accursed. *"But though we, or an angel from heaven, preach any other gospel unto you than that which we have preached unto you, let him be accursed." Galatians 1:8* This means such messages are not from God. The scripture also says, *"No wonder Satan himself disguises as an angle of light 2 Corinthians 11:14.* Please note that that scripture had been written long before these people started getting these angelic visitations and revelations supposedly from God. What the above examples and many more like them have done, is create confusion. The goal is to ensure opposition amongst ourselves thus, creating this confusing religious atmosphere we find in our world today.

In my personal experience over the years, I have come to believe strongly that mankind does have a strong inclination toward God. You only have to present something that seems godly to a human being and they will show respect and follow it if it needs following. I have seen people starving themselves, depriving themselves in the name of God. People are ready to die for what they believe is God's will for their lives. This had been the case from Bible times. Paul the Apostle wrote this about the Jews of his days:

"Brethren, my heart's desire and prayer to God for Israel is, that they might be saved. For I bear them record that they have zeal of God but not according to knowledge." Romans. 10:1-2.

Paul saw the dedication of the Jewish people back in his days. He saw how zealous they were, how they routinely followed doctrines they believed are from God. With a heavy heart, Paul stated that their zeal lacked the knowledge that is necessary to please God. *"Since they did not know the righteousness of God and sought to establish their own, they did not submit to God's righteousness." Romans 10:3.* Like the Jewish people described above, many of us in the world, sincerely believe in what we practice, what we have come to accept as God's ways for our lives, not giving any thought to question its authenticity at all. This dedication of man toward God shows only one thing; man is eager to please God, even if it means grabbling within uncertainties. Remember from the early part of this book, we saw that man's view of God is tainted because of sin. We also saw that all that man knows about God is another man's view of

God as he had been taught by yet, another man. This makes it a very fine playground for any Idea seemingly of God to sell.

The irony

The irony of this whole religious belief system is that most people believe there is only one God and that all religions serve Him. Justifying that concept by stating names ascribed to God for the various religious belief systems, names like God, Jehovah, Yahweh, Allah, etc. Arguing that they all come to Him from different angles. Then there is the contention amongst them about which religion is right and which is wrong. Interestingly each of them claims to be right and considers all the others wrong. And because each of them considers the others wrong, they believe that each of the other's worship is not acceptable to God, it is in vain.

The truth is, we do not serve the same God. What most religious and non-religious people don't know or are yet to know is the fact that there are many gods in this world. And that these gods are being worshipped by people. Remember I made mention of the prophets of Baal in the early pages of this book? And that God commanded not to have any gods before him? Yes, there are other gods and people worship them unconsciously. I say unconsciously because, I strongly believe that nobody in their right mind will knowingly and deliberately want to serve any other than God, the Creator. I am convinced that every religion except for a few people who openly worships the devil, intends to serve the God of heaven but when you examine our religious world with its contradictions how can you justify that? How can you say all religions are serving the same God when they contradict each other?

The fact that people do worship gods without knowing it can be deduced from a statement Jesus made to a woman he met at a well during His earthly ministry. The scripture records that Jesus was waiting by a well when a woman came to draw water from it. Jesus struck up a conversation with her that started with giving and receiving water from each other to ways of worship. During that conversation, one statement of Jesus stood out and it sheds light on the notion of the people's unconscious worship of gods.

> *"Jesus said to her, "Woman, believe Me, the hour is coming when you will neither on this mountain, nor in Jerusalem, worship the Father.* **You worship what you do not know; we know what we worship**, *for salvation is of the Jews. But the hour is coming, and now is, when the true worshipers will worship the Father in spirit and truth; for the Father is seeking such to worship Him. God is Spirit, and those who worship Him must worship in spirit and truth." John 4:21-23.*

In the words I underlined, Jesus told the woman something that is obscured from her and all her people who worshipped like her. The woman believed with all her heart that she and all the Samaritans were worshipping the God of heaven. This can be seen from her conversation with Jesus. *"The woman said unto him, Sir, I perceive that thou art a prophet. Our fathers worshipped in this mountain; and ye say that Jerusalem is the place where men ought to worship." John 4:19-20.* In those words, she did not only express her belief in God but also indicated that she believed that she was worshipping the same God as the Jews. She said her fathers worshipped on a particular mountain, but the Jews said Jerusalem was the place of worship. Jesus' response to the woman was very informative, amongst other things in His response, He told the woman she does not know what she had been worshipping. In that statement, Jesus was simply saying to her, that her worship was not to God Almighty whom she intended to worship but that it was rather directed to a god whom she was not aware of nor had acknowledged.

> *"Jesus said to her, "Woman, believe Me, the hour is coming when you will neither on this mountain, nor in Jerusalem, worship the Father.[22]* **You worship what**

you do not know; we know what we worship,
for salvation is of the Jews. John. 4:21-22.

Until her encounter with Jesus, she had not the slightest inclination in her mind about other gods, let alone the knowledge of her worshiping a different god. Had she known that, her conversation with Jesus might have read something like this, "our fathers worshipped our own god on that mountain but you, Jews worship your own in Jerusalem."

Like that woman, millions of people in our world today are in the same situation, not knowing what they are worshipping. Most religious people think we all serve the same God despite the contradictions in doctrines and this notion is far from the truth. The fact that there are many gods in the world seems hidden from people, and as long as this fact is obscured, people will always claim we all serve the same God and will not see the need to sieve through these belief systems to know the truth. This book is one such tool to give someone insight to know that we do not serve the same

God and is therefore necessary to sieve through to know how God speaks to us today, in order to speak back and relate to Him.

To emphasize this, I will draw attention to these facts recorded in scriptures. –

1. That people worshipped false gods. "*And it came to pass, as though it had been a trivial thing for him to walk in the sins of Jeroboam the son of Nebat, that he took as wife Jezebel the daughter of Ethbaal, king of the Sidonians; and **he went and served Baal and worshiped him.** 1Kings 16:31.* Here is a record of a wicked King that worshipped Baal a false god.

2. God warns about serving foreign gods. "*I am the LORD thy God, who brought thee out of the land of Egypt, out of the house of bondage. Thou shalt have no other gods before Me. Exodus 20:2.* If God warns about it, it is because it is so, He knows all things.

3. Miraculous powers are displayed that are not from God. We see the magicians of Pharaoh

performed the same miracle performed by Moses. *"But Pharaoh also called the wise men and the [b]sorcerers; so the magicians of Egypt, they also did in like manner with their [c]enchantments. 12 For every man threw down his rod, and they became serpents."* *Exodus 7:11.*

If these are true, what makes it hard to believe that people do worship other gods. I am imploring that we don't just shrug these facts or be in awe of its truth but rather to act on them. We all will face God someday. This is not to prove religious correctness; it is for the reader to be informed. Cross-check the facts in the scripture and observe the pieces of evidence in the world and make that decision.

A strategy in play

Chapter Five

Revealing God in Our Time

From all the chaos and confusion portrayed in our religious world, it is tempting to ask about God's whereabouts? Is He still with us? It may seem He had left mankind to fend, to scramble and search in uncertainty for Him. It may seem He had separated Himself from us perpetually. If that is not so, why all the confusion about God? Why all these different religious beliefs in the pursuit of God?

While it is logical to reason this way, it is very far from what God is doing. The Bible says God had been speaking throughout the ages, revealing Himself to man in two distinctive ways. In time past, through His prophets, but now in these last days, He is speaking to us through His Son. He used many prophets in various ways to talk to His people in the past. But in these last days, He is using only His Son!

"Long ago God spoke many times and in many ways to our ancestors through the prophets. And now in these final days, he has spoken to us through his Son…" Hebrews 1:1-2a

Most of the prophets God spoke through in the olden days, spoke a lot about His Son. They prophesied of His coming and of the tasks he was coming to accomplish. Those prophets acted like flag posts alongside a travel path to a specific destination. It seems the Son has a special task to do and therefore the many introductions by the prophets.

Why the Son?

The Prophet's Revelation of God was inadequate

In a previous chapter, I wrote of what I termed the hand me down revelation of God. How man only gets to know God based on how another man portrays Him. It is in that era that the prophets operated. They tried to pass on the revelation of God they had to their people as they themselves understood it. It should be noteworthy to know that even the prophets' minds can sometimes be clouded in perceiving God. An example of such is seen in Aaron. This Aaron was Moses's younger brother and his second in command in the things of God. Together they were leading the nation of Israel to a land God promised them. As they Journeyed Moses left them and went up a mountain by God's directions. In his absence, Aaron revealed his own perception by yielding to the people's cry and built them a god.

> *"When the people saw how long it was taking Moses to come back down the mountain, they gathered around Aaron. Come on they said, make us some gods who can lead us. We don't know what happened to this fellow Moses, who brought us here from the land of Egypt. So Aaron said, take the gold rings from the ears of your*

wives and sons and daughters and bring them to me. All the people took the gold rings from their ears and brought them to Aaron. Then Aaron took the gold, melted it down and molded it into the shape of a calf. When the people saw it, they exclaimed, O Israel, these are the gods who brought you out of the land of Egypt." Exodus 2:1-4.

This evidently confirmed that revealing God through the prophets was not full proof because it falls short of revealing God fully and had also produced a lot of misconstrued knowledge of Him. This is the reason why the Son stepped in to be the ultimate revealer of God.

The Son's Character makes Him Worthy

"And now in these final days, he has spoken to us through His Son…The Son radiates God's own glory and expresses the very character of God…Hebrews 1:2A-3A (New Living Translation). "Who being the brightness of his glory, and the

express image of his person." Hebrews 1:3A King James Version.

To drive in this point, I choose two versions of the Bible for this quote. The King James version says, *"the Son is the express image of God's person."* The living translation says, *"He expresses the very character of God"* Both of these versions use the word 'express' to define the Son in relation to God. It means, the Son expresses exactly who God is, simply put, the Son is a replica of God, their characters are cloned. This means every character that God possesses; His Son possesses as well. Characters like sinlessness, holiness, love, compassion and every other attribute of God. These were the very characters Adam our first father had in him with which he enjoyed fellowshipping with God because he knew and understood God perfectly. But he lost it all when he sinned and was only able to transfer the knowledge of God to his sons in his sinful state thus missing the mark. Adam's flawed character had been passed down to all mankind and so makes man unfit to reveal God as is, but the Son's character puts Him in a better position to do so.

Testimonies and Recommendations of the Son.

In job settings all over the world, there are two things that get people employed by most if not all employers, the potential employee's testimony and the recommendation of others on his behalf. When an employer puts out an ad for a job, people send in applications attaching their resume or curriculum vitae that serves as their testimony about the abilities and skills they possess for the position. They will also send in names of references who will give a recommendation to the prospective employer on their behalf. Like an employee would do, Jesus, who is the Son, testifies of Himself in many ways and have others who testified about Him even before He came to the world stage

Son's Testimony

Jesus was aware of the various religious practices and doctrines during His life on earth. He knew they were all proclaiming one way or the other to get to the God of heaven. He knew that despite their dedication, their sacrifices and piousness all in a bid to please God, they all had deep uncertainties of their hope for eternity. Jesus knew that every single one of these religious people were looking for the way to get to heaven and that they were doing so from within their religious teachings, following the founders and leaders of their religion. A religious atmosphere pretty much like ours today. It was amid that religious setting that He declared Himself to be the way to God. He said *"...I am the way the truth and the life: no man cometh unto the Father except by me." John 14:6.* He made that claim to His disciples who like every religious person were themselves not confident when it comes to how to get into heaven and Jesus wanted them to know and be assured. He encouraged them not to be worried but to be confident because He will go prepare a place for them and all of us who will become His disciples. No other religious leader before or after Jesus had made claims about mansions and going to prepare them for his or her followers.

> *"Let not your hearts be troubled: ye believe in God, believe also in me. In my Father's house are many mansions: if it were not so, I would have told you. I go to prepare a place for you. And If I go to prepare a place for you, I will come again and receive you unto myself; that where I am, there ye may be also. And wither I go ye know and the way ye know. John 14:1-4*

Claiming to be the only way was a big claim to make especially in a world with diverse belief systems that are all claiming to be a way to God. Jesus knew people will find it hard to believe that He is the only way to God like he claimed, so He backed it up with a few more claims; all of which he had proven. Like the one He made to Mary and Martha when He visited them. *"I am the resurrection and the life, he that believeth in me, though he were dead, yet shall he live." John 11:25.*

In this narrative, Jesus had gone to see Mary and Martha, who had just lost their brother Lazarus to death. When He was some distance away, Martha heard that He was coming to them, so she ran out to meet Him. When she met Him, she expressed her belief in the resurrection of the dead at the judgment. She had hoped to see her brother again only at the time of the resurrection and not before. *"Then Martha said to him, I know that he shall rise again in the resurrection at the last day." John 14:24.* When she said that, I believed, Jesus looked her straight in the eyes maybe wrap His arms around her and declared to her and all who were standing there that He is the resurrection and the life." *Jesus said to her, "I am the resurrection and the life. He who believes in Me, though he may die, he shall live." John 11:25.* Meaning, that He is the one who has the authority to bring people back to life, be it now or on the last day. He proved that by raising Lazarus a man that had died and had been in the tomb for four days back to life! Imagine the joy that that incident brought to the sisters and the awe that struck all the people that were around, both His followers and critics alike. He also fulfilled the "I am the resurrection and the life…" claim when He defeated death by coming back to life after He was killed, crucified horribly on the cross and buried. The only one of all the Prophets, Priests or messengers of God to do so! He is indeed the resurrection and the life. The scriptures record that at His resurrection, saints of old came out of their graves alive and walked the streets of Jerusalem. Proven to be exactly what He claimed to be, "the resurrection and the life…"

> *"Jesus, when he had cried again with a loud voice, yielded up the ghost. And behold, the veil of the temple was rent in twain from the top to the bottom; and the earth did quake, and the rocks rent; And the graves were opened; and many bodies of the saints which slept arose and they came out of the graves after his resurrection, and went into*

the holy city and appeared unto many. Mathew 27:50-53.

Here is something to ponder deeply. Every religion believes in the hereafter, and that the way to get there is after death. Every other religious leader had led their followers the best way they could have led them. They taught them how to live and relate to the God of heaven as they had perceived Him. And all of them, like every other man, had died or will die. Those that had died are still in their graves, those who are yet to die, will eventually die and will be in their graves as well. But for Jesus, it was not so, He rose from the dead on the third day as He promised, and He is alive! *"I am he that liveth and was dead and behold I am alive for evermore, Amen; and I have the keys of hell and of death."* Revelations *1:18* Let us pause and think hard about this, is it not God's intention to reconcile man to Himself? And is it not man's desire to get to God after this life? Remember, we are reasoning together to verify who is showing the way to the God of heaven, whom I believe every religious person intends to serve.

Now if someone that is supposed to lead you to a particular place got stuck at some point, and can't lead you anymore and then you hear about someone else going to that same place and this person went through every obstacle courageously and get to the desired destination, would it not seem a wise thing to follow that person? Think about that. God intends to lead man to heaven and man desires to get there but most of the people leading got stuck in the grave, but one man got up from the grave, took back His life and is currently in that very place. Think about it!

The third claim I will touch on is one that will give more clarity to the first two. Jesus said; *"I am the door, by me if any man enter in, he shall be saved and shall go in and out and find pasture." John 10:9.* Jesus said this when he was addressing the religious leaders who were bent on discrediting Him and the works he was doing on almost every occasion. At that incident, He had just healed a man that was born blind and that stirred the religious leaders to go on the offense against Him yet again. But as always, Jesus kept His composure and even reasoned with them making yet another claim, that He is the door by which one should enter. Jesus said whoever enters through Him, will go in and out and find pasture for their lives. This claim echoes the very first I choose to expound on, *"I am the way the truth and the life..." Jn:14:6a.* By many other claims did Jesus presented Himself to be the one through whom God is indeed revealed.

Testimonies of Others, Before and After Him

"Long ago God spoke many times and in many ways to our ancestors through the prophets....: Hebrews 1:1a

Long before Jesus stepped into the scene, there were prophets who had prophesied of His coming. Prophecies ranging from His virgin birth to the mission He was to accomplish on earth. Moses one of the greatest prophets in Bible times said this about His coming:

> *"The LORD your God will raise up for you a prophet like me from among you, from your fellow Israelites. You must listen to him For this is what you asked of the LORD your God at Horeb on the day of the assembly when you said, "Let us not hear the voice of the LORD our God nor see this great fire anymore, or we will die." The LORD said to me: What they say is good. I will raise up for them a prophet like you from among their fellow Israelites, and I will put my words in his mouth. He will tell them everything I command him. I myself will call to account anyone who does not listen to my words that the prophet speaks in my name Deuteronomy 18:15-19*

Moses was simply saying, that the prophet that God will raise should be listened to. In other words, His message should be a must heard, because they would be words of utmost importance and that God Himself will hold everyone accountable that will not listen to what this prophet would have to say. This prophet was identified as Jesus when Peter preached to the crowds after a lame man was healed in the name of Jesus.

Then Peter said, "Silver or gold I do not have, but what I do have I give you. In the name of Jesus Christ of Nazareth, walk." Taking him by the right hand, he helped him up, and instantly the man's feet and ankles became strong. He jumped to his feet and began to walk. Then he went with them into the temple courts, walking and jumping, and praising God... and that he may send the Messiah, who has been appointed for you—even Jesus.[21] Heaven must receive him until the time comes for God to restore everything, as he promised long ago through his holy prophets. [22] For Moses said, 'The Lord your God will raise up for you a prophet like me from among your own people; you must listen to everything he tells you.[23] Anyone who does not listen to him will be completely cut off from their people." Acts 3:6-8 & 20-23

The next great prophet that testified extensively of the Son was Isaiah. He spoke of His birth, how a virgin will conceive and will bring forth a son and that son will save his people from their sins. *"Therefore, the Lord himself shall give you a sign, Behold a virgin shall conceive, and bear a son and shall call his name Immanuel." Isaiah 7:14* …This scripture was fulfilled in Mathew's gospel.

> *"Now the birth of Jesus Christ was on this wise: When as his mother Mary was espoused to Joseph, before they came together, she was found with child of the Holy Ghost. [19] Then Joseph her husband, being a just man, and not willing to make her a public example, was minded to put her away privily. [20] But while he thought on these things, behold, the angel of the LORD appeared unto him in a dream, saying, Joseph, thou son of David, fear not to take unto thee Mary thy wife: for that which is conceived in her is of the Holy Ghost. [21] And she shall bring forth a son, and thou shalt call his name JESUS: for he shall save his people from their sins. [22] Now all this was done, that it might be fulfilled which was spoken of*

the Lord by the prophet, saying,[23] *Behold, a virgin shall be with child, and shall bring forth a son, and they shall call his name Emmanuel, which being interpreted is, God with us. Mathew 1:18-23*

Throughout the Old Testament, God ensures that the message of the coming of His Son saturates the scriptures. The Bible records a significant amount of testimonies about the coming of Jesus Christ in the scriptures. I could have gone on and on with one prophecy after another but that will take a whole book or two to do so. The few that I used here are to incite one's desire to read and research more in order to make a wise and informed decision. Remember, it is going to be you alone at the time of accountability and judgment before God.

One final point attesting to the fact that the Son is the method God is using to talk to man these days, is found recorded in the book of Jeremiah, God Himself said, He will make a new covenant with Israel and in that covenant, people will no longer teach other people to know God, but everyone will know Him.

> "Behold, the days come, saith the LORD, that I will make a new covenant with the house of Israel, and with the house of Judah: Not according to the covenant that I made with their fathers in the day that I took them by the hand to bring them out of the land of Egypt; which my covenant they brake, although I was an husband unto them, saith the LORD: But this shall be the covenant that I will make with the house of Israel; After those days, saith the LORD, I will put my law in their inward parts, and write it in their hearts; and will be their God, and they shall be my people. And they shall teach no more every man his neighbor, and every man his brother,

saying, Know the LORD*: for they shall all know me, from the least of them unto the greatest of them, saith the* LORD*: for I will forgive their iniquity, and I will remember their sin no more." Jerimiah 31,32A and 33A.*

Why did God decide to make a new covenant with Israel? Because He knew the first covenant or agreement did not work to perfection. There were major flaws in the revelation of God with the old method. Note that in the quoted scriptures, God said, everyone will know Him and that no one will teach his brother to know God.

Looking through the scriptures, we discover that the above-quoted scripture was fulfilled in Jesus as recorded in the book of Hebrews. The writer's argument was to let his audience; the believers of his day, see and understand the new covenant God had made with Israel; and for them to grasp the importance and benefits of it. He wrote: -

"But now Jesus, our High Priest, has been given a ministry that is far superior to the old priesthood, for he is the one who mediates for us a far better covenant with God, based on better promises.[7] If the first covenant had been faultless, there would have been no need for a second covenant to replace it. But when God found fault with the people, he said: **"The day is coming, says the LORD, when I will make a new covenant with the people of Israel and Judah. [9]This covenant will not be like the one I made with their ancestors when I took them by the hand and led them out of the land of Egypt. They did not remain faithful to my covenant, so I turned my back on them, says the LORD. [10] But this is the new covenant I will make with the people of Israel on that day, says the LORD: I will put my laws in their minds, and I will write them on their hearts. I will be their God, and they will be my people. [11] And they will not need to teach their neighbors,**

**nor will they need to teach their relatives,**[d]
**saying, 'You should know the LORD.' For**
**everyone, from the least to the greatest, will**
**know me already.** _And I will forgive their_
wickedness, and I will never again remember their
sins."[e] _13 When God speaks of a "new" covenant, it_
means he has made the first one obsolete. It is now out of
date and will soon disappear." Hebrews 8:6-14

The underlined portion is the quote from the old
testament where God first promised it through
Jeremiah the Prophet. There are very many more I can
use to testify of the Son's worthiness, but these few I
believe suffices.

How to Know God in these Last Days

From the scriptures we've learned that man will
no longer teach his brother to know God any longer,
this might cause one to wonder if it is over for man's
participation in sharing the knowledge of God? And if
that is so, how will everyone know God? What method

is used to do so and what role do we have to play in fulfilling this method? The truth is man has always been, and still is God's means to accomplish His goals on earth this one inclusive; only this time around, man does not do the teachings, man introduces the next man to Jesus, and He will do the teaching Himself, this way, the hand me down effect is none effective.

My Summation.

Without a doubt in my mind, I am totally convinced that everyone, religious or not has an idea of the hereafter. People believe in life after death and this belief is one factor that had driven and still drives us to be in one religious setting or the other. Following teachings and practices of such religions with the intention to serve God to the best of our abilities in ways, we were either introduced to or ways we discovered ourselves, with one hope in mind, to make the hereafter and live with God forever. If that is not a good desire, tell me what is? But the trouble is, we live in a world of a variety of religious beliefs and practices. It is evident that we have more religions that one can count all proclaiming God but are mostly contradictory to each other. Because of this, we find ourselves living in a chaotic religious atmosphere. How can one get to know the truth?

Examining the two ways described by which God had spoken to man, in the olden days through His prophets and in these last days, through His Son, I had laid out an argument that can help one make an informed decision. God had meticulously given ample testimonies that separate His Son from everyone else. Looking at this historic incident surrounding the coming Messiah, one should wonder why? Why was His birth announced? Why did angels celebrate his birth?

> *Now there were in the same country shepherds living out in the fields, keeping watch over their flock by night And behold, an angel of the Lord stood before them, and the glory of the Lord shone around them, and they were greatly afraid. Then the angel said to them, "Do not be afraid, for behold, I bring you good tidings of great joy which will be to all people. For there is born to you this*

day in the city of David a Savior, who is Christ the Lord. And this will be the sign to you: You will find a Babe wrapped in swaddling cloths, lying in a manger." Luke 2:8-14

And suddenly there was with the angel a multitude of the heavenly host praising God and saying: "Glory to God in the highest, And on earth peace, goodwill toward men!"

Is his birth the first on the world stage? If not, what is this male child's birth that it had to be reported ahead of time. Why is the world's calendar year marked before and after Him? Why did He make so many claims, all of which He fulfilled? His was so because God wants Him to reveal Himself to man in a very personal way. The scripture says the Son is the express image of God, He is God's look-alike who came down to reveal God to us.

"The Son radiates God's own glory and expresses the very character of God..." Hebrews 1:3a

"Christ is the visible image of the invisible God. He existed before anything was created and is supreme over all creation," Colossians 1:15 As the scriptures says, Jesus is the visible image of God, He expresses God's characters in absolution. Something that no other man can do. He can do so because He knows God the Father through and through and so He is in place to come down and reveal God in a personal way no other could.

My Challenge to You!

In life, we are faced with many challenges and of all the challenges we are faced with, the greatest of all is to know and live for God, yet we take it lightly for the most part. We are not even cognizance of the fact that knowing God is the biggest challenge for our lives. We are in a culture or a system that is plagued by man's shortsightedness and gullibility. Mankind's attitude toward God is casual, we call on Him only when we need Him. We take things for granted and have become gullible to many things. We do not examine statements or do the arithmetic to deduce facts from imaginations, to get what's true from what's not. I am therefore challenging you to reason along with me. Let's reason Jesus, His claims, His accomplishments and Promises.

In the chapter above the immediate one, I pose some thought-provoking questions, some that are meant to let the reader ponder deeply, to separate fictions and imaginations from what is indeed real. In this chapter, I will like to further deepen those thoughts and juggle our brains with a few more verified facts about Jesus. The Bible records the very many miracles He did on earth, and these miracles were a testimony of His uniqueness. At one point He even asked the religious world of His day to believe Him because of the works he did.

"If I do not the works of my Father, believe me not. But if I do, though ye believe not me, believe the works: that ye may know and believe that the Father is in me and I am in." John 10:37-38.

No one had ever done what Jesus did on earth. Is that not worth looking at? Is it not worth some consideration when it comes to how we relate to God?

Does that not count at all? Must one really find their own way despite the uniqueness of Jesus? For it is recorded in scriptures that, Jesus did many more works that were not recorded. *"And there are also many other things which Jesus did, the which, if they should be written everyone, I suppose that even the world itself could not contain the books that should be written, Amen." John 21:25*

Jesus also made very many promises to His disciples but for this thought-provoking part of this book, I will focus on just one of His promises. Jesus promised His disciples that He will send another Comforter to them, the Holy Spirit.

"Nevertheless I tell you the truth; it is expedient for you that I go away: for if I go not away, the Comforter will not come unto you; but if I depart, I will send him unto you....Howbeit when he the Spirit of Truth is come, he will guide you into all truth...John 16:7 & 13A.

This promise is acknowledged as been fulfilled by at least two major religious bodies. For the Christians or believers in the Lord Jesus, it was an event that occurred at a yearly Jewish religious festival called Pentecost.

> *"When the day of Pentecost was fully come, they were all with one accord in one place. And suddenly there came a sound from heaven as of a rushing mighty wind, and it filled all the house where they were sitting. And there appeared unto them cloven tongues like as of fire, and it sat upon each of them. And they were filled with the Holy Ghost and began to speak with other tongues, as the Spirit gave them utterance." Acts 2:1-4.*

The other religion that embraces Jesus's promise of the Holy Spirits are Muslims. They believe an angel named Gabriel is the Holy Spirit. Surah 2:97; Surah 16 102. Both Surahs speaks of how the Quran was brought down. While who they refer to as the Holy Spirit differs from Who the Christians know Him to be, the fact of the matter is they believed in Jesus's promise. Notice that the two major religions in the world believed in Jesus' promise, that also gives credibility to Jesus's claims.

Now here is my argument concerning this. It is a fact that these two religions believed in the promised Holy Spirit. They believe He will come after Jesus departs from the earth just like Jesus said it would be. However, these two religious bodies differ on who they Identify as Holy Spirit. And because they differ it means, one of them got it right the other did not. One identifies the Holy Spirit as Jesus promised, the other did not. So how can one know which of these two religions identifies the Holy Spirit correctly? To do so one will have to go back to the original source and see what else was said concerning the coming of the Holy Spirit. Jesus who said, He will send the Holy Spirit did say the things that the Spirit will be doing once He come down to earth. Examine these sayings and check to see where they are being carried out. Below are some of the sayings of Jesus concerning the Holy Spirit.

"But the Advocate, the Holy Spirit, whom the Father will send in my name, will teach you all things and will remind you of everything I have said to you." John 14:26

"On one occasion, while he was eating with them, he gave them this command: "Do not leave Jerusalem, but wait for the gift my Father promised, which you have heard me speak about. For John baptized with water, but in a few days you will be baptized with ⌐the Holy Spirit." Act 1:4-5. Not long after that encounter, according to scriptures, the disciples experienced what we know to be the baptism of the Holy Spirit as Jesus promised. *"When the day of Pentecost was fully come, they were all with one accord in one place. And suddenly there came a sound from heaven as of a rushing mighty wind, and it filled all the house where they were sitting. And there appeared unto them cloven tongues like as of fire, and it sat upon each of them. And they were filled with the Holy Ghost and began to speak with other tongues, as the Spirit gave them utterance." Acts 2:1-4.*
This is seen and believed as the fulfilment of the promised Holy Spirit.

In wrapping up, I hope you find this book interesting, thought-provoking and helpful. I hope it makes you understand a lot more and it will help you make the needed decision for life.

"And if it seem evil unto you to serve the Lord, choose you this day whom ye will serve; whether the gods which your fathers served that were on the other side of the flood, or the gods of the Amorites, in whose land ye dwell; but as for me and my house, we will serve the Lord!" Joshua 24:15

Made in the USA
Middletown, DE
20 May 2020